A TAIWAN RHAPSODY

The Alliance of the Weak

Volume 1

Written by INFINITY A

In memory of my grandmother

To those **kidnapped by** *success,*

hope you will perceive **what matters**

in life **to** reconstruct **humanity**

in this dire hour

by experiencing **the emotions** in fictions

that *inspire* **reality.**

我我の社会に合理的外観を与えるものは実はその不合理の——その余りに甚しい不合理の為ではないであろうか？

芥川龍之介

We cloak the society with ration because its irrationality is way too irrational, isn't it?

Ryunosuke Akutagawa

1

Ming woke up.

Another day of suffering he thought. His body got pulled up by a habitual force. He sprang up as if someone was whipping him to move.

The first thing he did in the morning would be in the bathroom. He was not the kind of person who would practice personal grooming to start a refreshing day. No, he was not. There, he would look at himself in the mirror, checking if there was any physical flaw on his pathetic human flesh. He thought a tiny balding patch on his head would make his day.

Mother. His face still looked pale and untainted, hair thick and much.

Exhaling a long calm breath of desperation, he asked the weary soldier in the reflection,

"When will it be your turn to win?"

His voice registered in a neutral zone, but the rounded fist had already taken the preemptive strike to demonstrate his uncompensated rage.

He didn't stop the attack until a drill of scolding abomination piercing through the war wall:

Stop the fucking noise, motherfucker. Are you trying to tear down the whole building? You moron...

Ming roared at the top of his lungs as if it was his last struggle before trampled by a fleet of nervy wild animals. Then, on the cheap synthetic wood that had comparted the entire building floors into dozens of compact single rooms, he culminated his heroic fight with one last crushing pound. Pain forsook hot pursuit.

"Fuck you. You do this every morning. Been warning you about this hundreds of times. Fuck you, I'm gonna make you pay for the ghostly noise you make all morning. Come out, you fuck. If I don't give you a lesson today, I'm a fucking loser turtle..."

Having heard the neighbor storm out and hammer on his door, he sneered. *The wall is surely thin...*

He was again betrayed by the reflection in the mirror. He had always been. In some good days, he could see his face with reddish, uneven skin resembling the Martian surface—the kind of face that spoke genetic skin allergies or systemic lupus erythematosus, the kind that was envied by most people in Taiwan—but of course, these were the faces he could only see in his imaginations. The kind of face he suffered from looking at every day was the look of slave, despair, and inevitable tragedy. Failure was what his face said and what most people read. There was not a day he would quit grieving for his flawless look.

"Yeah, you better not come out. Don't let me see you, or I'll so give you a piece of my mind. You will pay for what you've done one day, you so will. If you think you can get out of this, I will change my last name into yours."

BOOM. Stomping fiercely on Ming's door, the neighbor retreated, "**Fuck!**"

Ming could detect his neighbor's steps were rushing away. *Pity, also a poor guy bullied by this ghost island.* He knew sooner or later the neighbor would be dragged away by the leash of time. *We are surely tamed underdogs...*

Insusceptible to the commotion he perceived meaninglessly comical, Ming aimed carefully the tattoo stickers at his cheeks.

Like the dike boy, he also hoped that whatever lay against his fingers could stay in place forever. *Rest 3 minutes.* He read the note on the package and checked his phone—he was allowed exactly 3 minutes to rest the tattoos on his face if he wanted to clock his work card on time.

He stepped out of the bathroom, eyeing the room humbly furnished with the bed he found hard like a rock, the stacked chair he never had the privilege to lay on, and the worn closet he picked up from trash piles, stuffing with objects but clothes.

All his belongings, asserting legitimate inherency as if they were the sole successors of the room, took over nearly most of the space, leaving his living area the corner of a single bed and a slim passage way revealed in the sea of mounted boxes of instant noodles and canned food and bottled water and toilet papers and the like. The room, he thought, was never meant to be lived in by people like him. He had to compete for space with items that kept him survived.

The books, and only the books—the symbol of education leading to exciting life opportunities— were the guests to this room that could receive his most hearted hospitality. As he browsed the books sleeping face-up in peace on his bed accompanied by a conspicuous mark of human arch, he speculated his life could be turned around if everything worked exactly like he planned for today. He speculated that soon he would farewell his prison days—the time he would curl hopelessly on his half bed, exhausted by the countdown of his release.

Ming swiftly pulled out a white shirt from the clothes hill that had rooted into the legs of chair. *Nothing comes more suitable than a white shirt for today.* He flipped off the parasite crumbles, deliberately buttoned himself from the way up, convinced he was too one of the gentlemen he saw from old movies.

He wanted to look good and impeccable today.

2

Ming dashed out.

He dashed out before he was too shepherded by the staff of time constraint. He knew he had risked a few more minutes to put another sticker on his forehead. He wanted his face to speak perfection even covered by a mask.

It was his turn now to race against time.

Living on the outskirts of an industrial park, however close Ming dwelt from work, spending forty minutes to work was a complete torture when his legs were the only vehicles he could claim as his mobile estate. It wasn't like he never thought about getting a bike before. He did, a long time ago.

However, considering no sound mind nowadays would do cycling on the street and serve their lungs as free air purifiers, he would rather walk in a pollution hotspot and avoid breathing hastily. Moreover, as the demand in bicycle market dropped, those survived redirected their business producing ornamental bicycles—the more vintage the look, the higher the price.

It was common to see a wealthy Taiwanese household exhibiting a rusty, old bicycle imprinted with a GIANT logo instead of paintings on the wall— a local interior design trend boomed only decades ago. Any broken bike with a GIANT logo would speak for its collectible self. The logo sticker business, hysterically, became more rampant than ever.

Bicycle, as it used to be an equipment for sport, had transcended into an icon of social status in Taiwan. It was impossible for Ming to find one that was both for use and affordable.

Chian duo, shi shao, li jia jin had long been the three pillars, the holy trinity, the perfect combination of Taiwanese dream jobs: lots money, little work, near home; yet, Ming understood clearly sometimes living near to where you work in a time like this wasn't always a perk, especially for someone like him, doing what he did. Most tech engineers would commute for thirty minutes in their cozy, metal boxes of cars from a farther neighborhood without the direct exposure to industrial pollution.

Chian duo, shi shao, li jia jin
錢多，事少，離家近

It wasn't long before Ming arrived at the main road where several breakfast vendors clustered along the curbs. The main road was the only passage leading to the core of industrial park, and whoever slaved or bossed inside would have to stop and purchase their first meal there.

And *there* survived no discrimination. Car owners, riders, walkers all waited their turns to place orders, following the law of first come, first served. Those who possessed would be stripped of their possessions.

Cars and scooters were halted in disarray.

Once those who possessed came out of their cars, down from their scooters, they were nothing different from those who walked.

Thus, buying breakfast on his way to work was one of the few moments Ming felt he was treated equally. The breakfast vendors never bothered to notice how you came here because no matter what kind of wheels you sat behind, you only bought a portion for one.

Ming surveyed the people in lines having their helmets on, wondering whether they kept them for the sake of saving time or saving face. *Pretentious bastards.*

There were normally food stands selling fried noodles, buns, egg pancakes and many others that were long considered typical Taiwanese breakfast. The pride for food each Taiwanese shared, rich or poor, was perhaps the single collective culture succeeded from their disparate predecessors.

The variety of options lured before Ming.

But he only had eyes for fan-tuan. He thought nothing else except sticky rice could fed him long enough to skip lunch.

fan-tuan 飯糰

"What do you want, handsome?" asked a discharging loud volume through the mask. Ming felt a flush of gratification. He knew the vendor probably just said it out of commercial flattery. It still gave him quite a confidence boost about his look which he really wanted to be good today. He was pleased about the rash-like look on his face he had fashioned earlier.

"A tuna combo, black tea, large, half sugar, no ice." Ming told the vendor.

"Add egg?"

"No egg," Ming answered after a quick peep into his wallet.

Not unlike their SOP for transactions, when the food package was delivered *mechanically* to his hands, he poked through the plastic lid with a sharply tipped plastic straw, and took a good sip from the translucent petroleum–based product. Taken out of, perhaps, instincts or acquired habits, his actions were too streamlined to be spot any unnatural flow. The plastics, having become an inseparable culture of contemporary lives, were adopted unconditionally due to its convenience by people who selfishly saw efficiency as a way to prevent waste. People forgot sometimes convenience could be producing more wastes. But sadly, Ming and most others were the majority that didn't get the irony.

His mind, constructed by bricks of industrial logic, simply interpreted the item he bought a short recharge of sugar that would power him just enough to speed his journey to make up for the time he lost.

Having no second to waste, he was back on track after sipping few satisfying placebos.

Run, run, run, as fast as he can. But the wheels always caught him, he was only a two-legged man.

The scooters and cars were always faster no matter how fast he ran. Dozens of vehicles had surpassed Ming since he raced on the road.

Mother-gan, he damned. *How come this traffic light always turns red on me? Is it fucking broken?* He was infuriated to have been treated unequally, especially by abrupt instructions, or to be exact, rules. He glared in raging silence at the chunky metallic butts —the lucky butts that had escaped the spank of prejudiced social rulings—shrinking in distance as they drove away.

He looked to the left at the late-coming vehicles gradually rallying in rows behind the red light, and within seconds it had become a troop of two-wheel soldiers and tanks that gave Ming an unspeakable pressure.

Lucky bastards.

He didn't remember the last and only time he was on one of these *things*. He didn't remember who offered him the ride, either. By law, he was never allowed to own a scooter (let alone to ride on one) or a car.

He was used to detaching himself from any merry expectations, knowing the leviathan of society would cruelly drown him with her tentacles in the sea. He learnt not to lift up his hope, not even a fool's hope, for feeling the blast in his veins once more when he first experienced getting somewhere without deploying his legs. His life was never lighter on the top of the moving wheels. He thought that must have been what freedom felt like.

He didn't want to lift up his hope...until now.

The scooter army marched when the light sparked green. Ming sprinted without reserving any of his momentum but it only took seconds before he could only be seen in the rear view mirrors.

Time is money. He learned it by facts that it was not merely a saying. It was reality, a hard rock reality that would grind him, juice him until nothing left to be squeezed—if he came in late for work. For every ten minutes late, his paycheck would be deducted by NTD 100, no cap limit. He understood clearly that for people like him, they didn't have the luxury to lose their time. He must make hastes. *Time is money.*

"Ming," someone yelled from behind. "You still here? Someone is going to do free labor today. You better hurry." The rider slowed down to tease Ming and then gusted away.

Mother-gan. It was Ming's supervisor.

3

8:07.

Ming was delighted that his paycheck was secure today. He was proud, even, to have three extra minutes before the work bell rang.

How lucky. He thought to himself while he couldn't stop coughing. His mask was still on, and he could barely catch his breath. The non-stop coughing didn't ruin his joy at all. In fact, when the work bell rang, all he felt was how great he managed to run so fast although he used up all the spared time to cough.

"Nice work with the tattoos," Bai tapped Ming's shoulder and exclaimed in the changing room. "I told you I make the best tattoo stickers in Taichung. They look so real that if you tell anyone you have type 1 skin, no one would ask you for your med card."

Soaking in sweat, Ming swallowed his last itchy burst down the throat and took off his mask. "Well thanks, I hope they won't come off later today," Ming still felt distant with Bai who just got distributed to the factory three months ago.

"Don't you worry. Your date is going to be thrilled. Remember. Bai's quality is the best quality in Taiwan."

Ming replied with a polite but soulless smile, thinking how Bai just levelled up his craftsmanship from top of the city to the top of the country at ease. He was both impressed and reserved by Bai's bold confidence.

"Tell you what. If it weren't for the environment, I would have become a world class fashion designer already. If only I were born limp or with any type 1 conditions, I wouldn't be stuck here slaving my ass like hell."

Ming rolled up his eyes with a hint of contempt. "You and me, Bai. You and me. We all think we could be something else, having better lives but that's how it works here. That's the environment," Ming knew he had been saying this for countless times, especially to someone like Bai, unacquainted and whiny.

He always gave the same speech every time he received the ear bombs from someone complaining how their lives would have been wonderful if they were born decades earlier, or how would they have succeeded if it weren't for the *environment*. It always drained him to listen to those woe and moan.

Never had he once felt sympathetic or it's-not-that-bad-for-me when people told him somewhat more misfortunate encounters. For Ming, to jibber jabber your tragic life meant waste-of-tongue, and to actually feel better by those jibber jabber meant sheer stupidity. Because by the end of the day, whether you liked it or not, you were going to be the same pathetic person despite comprehending the existence of people in peril. *It wouldn't change a goddamn thing if I say otherwise*, he thought.

Ming understood clearly for people like Bai and him would always be the helpless minority even if they could stick together. He refused to live in the illusion of we-are-not-alone.

So he had no better things to say. It wasn't like he accepted the way how the environment had determined his future. No, he never did. He once fought hard against the world around him before he found there was no way to win the war unless you joined the world. It had been evident to him that the ticket to the world is to wed a handicap or become one. He felt pity for those fools who fantasized to crawl out their shitholes with their full limbs.

"Fuck the environment. The environment is unfair," Bai slammed his locker.

"You realized that just now?"

"No, of course I know it is unfair. It's just I want to prove that even against all odds, I have the ability to achieve my dreams. I want to be made proud."

"That's why you are selling these stickers?"

"Yes. If more and more people using my products, I will be both rich and famous."

Ming paused and surveyed the cheeky boy in front of him, "You're 14, right?"

"Yes, will turn 15 next month."

"I see," Ming nodded his head and gave Bai a polite and soulless smile.

"What are you guys still doing here? Get your asses moving and start working!" they heard from the next room where their supervisor was gushing at the poor souls with the power they all thought undeserved. They knew, however, they had to listen to him because his title pretty much guaranteed so. Although inside their brain theater, they were each raising how-dare-you, you-useless-prick, and fuck-you-who-do-you-think-you-are protesting signs, they knew if they didn't move their asses now, they would be whirled into his next growling tornado.

They quickly put on the clean room suits and new masks before entering the workshop.

The one-time mask Ming wore to work was already all sweaty and clung with visible greyish stuff. The mask, despite serving for less than an hour, was retired with recognition for fulfilling its duties. Say, if masks could think, would they be wondering whether they had seen better days knowing they would be thrown away eventually?

It was a hot summer day on June 4th, 2089.

4

The factory where Ming and Bai worked in Taichung belonged to tsmc, the once most revered company in Taiwan.

Taiwan Semiconductor Manufacturing Company.

It was established in the last century and had remained the pride of Taiwanese industrial success in the past generations.

Ming remembered his grandfather told him if you ever got your ticket to work in tsmc, your life claimed victory. You would be paid with better incomes, given higher social ranks, treated with more discounts when shopping if you showed your tsmc employee card. His grandfather was an engineer in tsmc, and he was proud to have 20% off from the products in Apple stores back in his days.

It was a commonly agree-upon consensus that tsmc was the backbone of Taiwan's economy ... until the 30s.

Ming stood in front of the production line repeating the same action, the action requiring full focus and precision but numbing one's mind. He did the same tasks from 8 to 5, Monday to Sunday, no vacations all year long. He was rewarded 45K a month if he didn't ask for a personal day, or a sick leave, and could keep his defect rate under 1%.

He could have 45K at his best.

In a society where the cheapest noodles in night markets cost NTD 100, and the average rent for a single room in habitable districts was 60K, Ming had no choice but to live in a place with factories situating right next to his building and foul smell coming from each direction. He fed on cheap, dirty food stands, and slept in a 4-story warehouse-turned-dormitory with 80 something other workers cramming in their own tiny space they called home.

Ming knew it by heart he could never claim victory as the way his grandfather did. The time had changed, so had the environment. But working under the same name made him believe he shared some of his former glory despite being a production line worker.

He had fought hard to earn his place in tsmc. From his first distributed post in a chemical plant, he worked relentlessly to collect as many credits as he could to one day choose the post based on his will. He succeeded. He succeeded after 10 years of excellent performance, a feat that only few had achieved.

He applied for the permanent position in tsmc two years ago, and to never leave this post was the closest way to his limited victory before he could unfold a new life chapter; at least, this was what he chose to believe.

Taiwan Now and Then

Ghost island, as the locals already called it in sarcasm in the beginning of the century, is what the world think of Taiwan nowadays. The once known country for its friendly people, delicious street food, and beautiful nature was wiped out from the map by its own hands of economic pursuit.

The once top of the four Asian dragons.

The once lighthouse of democracy.

All these memories were created in the time when you could still breathe freely, even during global pandemic in the 20s. The truth is if you ever pay a visit to Taiwan now (the chances are you won't), you wouldn't feel safe without putting on a mask (or two). While the masks could block you from some invisible toxins, they couldn't block you from the sight of ghosts possessing the people—the ghosts that consume critical brains, and turn the living souls into mindless walking zombies.

How Taiwan became a ghost island was a foreseeable but sadly irreversible future.

From 2040s, people in Taiwan started to criticize the impacts brought by the economic development built heavily on manufacturing. Some people blamed the government for the ever-enlarging wealth gaps between the rich and the poor because they believed it was the government's fault to emphasize the economy on the least efficient industry.

Hence, there were experts argued that Taiwan had contributed the most capitals, labors, and technologies in the worldwide chains of semiconductor industry but had received the lowest revenue because Taiwan offered the most boring part of the services that did not require innovation and creativity.

It wasn't difficult for Taiwanese people to fall for mere rhetoric, of course, as long as some daunting incidence came along. When the average salary of tsmc engineers could no longer afford buying a two-roomed apartment in livable areas if they didn't spend 95 percent of their income on a 30-year mortgage in the late 40s, people found it reasonable to conclude a causal relation between the wealth gap and the wrong ante put on the semiconductor industry despite common sense would dictate a complex of factors at play.

tsmc, and to the extent of the whole semiconductor manufacturing industry had then become the prey of public predators urging answers to their problems. And that was even during the time when people celebrated the liberation of knowledge thanks to the boom of shared information on the internet and social media in the early 21st century. Ironically, knowing didn't lead to thinking.

When people know, people stop thinking.

And people in Taiwan had apparently stopped questioning now that they were fed with immediate answers. Until bigger problems arrive, tsmc would continue taking blames while manufacturing industry still accounted largely for Taiwan's economy.

However, one thing was for sure, the over-populated factories that supported the survival of the commoners had taken tolls on Taiwanese people. The mixed pollution coming out from the millions of factory's chimneys and pipes that disregarded the regulation of environmental protection had caused more and more new-born infants with innate genetic defects.

The poisonous chemical wastes from manufacturing IC parts, mobile cars, fabrics, or heavy metals had found their way to stay permanent residents in Taiwanese flesh through air, water and soil. 8 out of 10 babies suffered from physical deforms, skin diseases, or brain damaged since birth in 2060s. By 2075, the qualified workforce among the population consisted of only 10 percent, and it has kept decreasing each year.

It didn't take long before born with physical suffering had turned into a blissful endowment. To replenish the shortage of labor in menial works in still incredibly many factories, the law mandates that once citizens in wholesome health condition turn 14, they would be put to workforce prioritized for manufacturing needs after finishing their terms in Special Education Camp—all the condition-free kids would acquire their basic trainings, the ones essential to the operation of factory machines and state machines, in the course of 8-year discipline from the age of six.

As for the people born with genetic defects, they become the new majority occupying positions in governments, banks, hospitals, offices, shops, art studios, and places that do not require to be exposed to industrial toxins or harsh working environments. They are the new dominators rising in bulks that could access to different life choices. A deformed figure, or horrible-looking skins sensitive to exterior stimulation all speak immunity from working as low-income rednecks. These ghastly appearances in foreigner's eyes are now the presentation of beauty, hope, and happiness in Taiwan.

The key to *success* has been remolded under the great shift in demographic structure. The once considered majority has now become the minority, the power now the oppressed, and the strong now the weak.

Written by Infinity A

Infinity A is a Taiwanese writer who seeks the meaning of life in creation. We know nothing more about him/her for the moment.

Illustrated by Sumit Roy

Sumit Roy, aka Scorpy, lives with wife Arpita and daughter Sian in Basirhat, India.

Graduated in physics, Scorpy pursues drawing career for his love for books. He has been awarded for Bengali comics & Bengali webzine illustration.

ISBN: 978-626-97853-0-8

Middle Earth LLC, B1., No. 181, Sec. 2, Taiwan Blvd., West Dist.,
Taichung City, Taiwan.

www.m-earth.org